C. Boulanger is a retired graphic designer who remains an active visual artist, exhibiting her artwork at Gallery 121 in Belleville, Ontario, and at the Belleville Art Association. She enjoys family and friends, painting, teaching, and traveling. Her work is represented in private and permanent collections including Crayola Crayons (Binney and Smith), the Scarborough Board of Education, the Corby Library Gallery, the Georgetown Helson Gallery, the John and Gisela Sommer collection, and the University of Guelph Macdonald Stewart Art Centre. She has also illustrated *Hooray for Today* and *Sunflakes and Snowshine*, two children's books written by Fran Newman and published by North Press (Scholastic-Tab Publications).

ANIMAL ABC

FOR CHILDREN OF ALL AGES

C. Boulanger

AUSTIN MACAULEY PUBLISHERS™

LONDON • CAMBRIDGE • NEW YORK • SHARJAH

Copyright © C. Boulanger 2024

Ordering Information
Quantity sales: Special discounts are available on quantity purchases by corporations, associations, and others. For details, contact the publisher at the address below.

Publisher's Cataloging-in-Publication data
Boulanger, C.
Animal ABC for Children of All Ages

ISBN 9798886932362 (Paperback)
ISBN 9798886932379 (ePub e-book)

Library of Congress Control Number: 2023922849

www.austinmacauley.com/us

First Published 2024
Austin Macauley Publishers LLC
40 Wall Street, 33rd Floor, Suite 3302
New York, NY 10005
USA

mail-usa@austinmacauley.com
+1 (646) 5125767

With love to my beautiful family.

WHAT DO YOU SAY FOR A?

Hark! Hark!
The AARDVARK and the Lark
could never bark
at a Shark
in a park or in the dark.
Lark in the sky...
What happened to the Lark?

Say 'hello'
to mellow fellow
who is known as
ARMADILLO.
Here he rests
upon a pillow
eating yellow jello
while

Andy the ANTELOPE
eats a cantaloupe
and

an APE in a cape
eats a grape.

Hooray for 'A'!

Pierre the BEAR,
sat in a chair,
in his underwear
eating a pear
with his foot
in the air.
He talked to the Hare.
'I've had a scare'
cried the BEAR
'There's a tear in
the chair!'

'Where?'
asked the Hare.
'Right there!'
said the BEAR.
'Well – repair the tear!'
replied the Hare.

Soon a fly
wearing a tie
went by in the sky.
'Would you care
to share my
lovely pear?'
asked the BEAR.

In June,
a maroon BABOON
on his honeymoon
and a Raccoon
and a Loon
all crooned a tune
on a dune
to the moon
Alas...
The tune was ruined
too soon.

The fly replied:
'I only eat pie
and I only drink rye,'
and he sighed
and said goodbye.

c

My CAT Pat
is an acrobat.
He wears a hat
like a diplomat.
His friend the Rat
is an aristocratic brat
who lives on a mat
with a maniac Gnat.

HO! HO!
'How low can you go?'
asked the
slow-witted CROW
from Ohio.
He didn't know
which way to go
so he asked Joe
the yo-yo pro
from Buffalo.

Larry, the merry CANARY
will carry a berry
from the dairy
while, Chubby the CUB
sits in a tub
and orders a sub.

Mrs. Crane
lived down the lane
and had a
very quiet brain.
Although she was plain
and a bit of a pain, she was
extremely vain,
wore a chain and
walked with a cane.
She'd sit on a
a plane and flirt
with the captain.

Pow! Pow!
Brown COW and Sow
had a terrible row –
but they can
take a fine bow
because it's over now.

Kyle, the wild CROCODILE,
from the NILE
will not smile
if he has to
walk a MILE
on
TILE.

D

Did you hear this year that a very queer DEER is the
new cashier
at the rear of a pier?
It is clear and I fear
it appears he will cheer
in your ear
for a beer...

I am agog
that happy DOG
and a friendly Frog, drank cold eggnog
then went for a jog
on a log in the fog
with Mr. Hog.

After tea,
the DONKEY
and the Monkey
got all wonky
when they danced
to honky-tonky
SO

they sat in a bunk
with a Chipmunk
and a Skunk
until that bunk
went KER-PLUNK!
They sent that bunk
that now was junk
to the dump
with a monk.

E

Is it legal to be an EAGLE
OR
a regal BEAGLE
OR
a SEAGULL?
AND is it lawful to be just awful?

Neil the EEL
made a deal
in the field
with a SEAL
named Lucille
to congeal
all their meals
with
orange peels.

Bella the ELEPHANT thought it was relevant
to assist her Aunt Pelican who'd lost her
smell again.
It was restored with an elixir of rose
made just for her nose.
YES!
ELEPHANT helped Aunt Pelican
recover her elegant smell again.

F

Meanwhile...
Freddy the FISH
just wishes
to abolish
the dishes!

A FAWN named John
after he yawns
on the lawn
is gone
at dawn

AND

FRANCIS the Fox
walks on the rocks
in his socks
near the phlox.

He talks to the Hawk
on the dock
who just
sits and gawks
at the FOX.

G

Adele the GAZELLE
fell in the dell
on her way
to the well.
She'll use her cell
and her yell
until the town bell
will tell she fell.

PLEASE NOTE:
The GOAT! The GOAT!
He wears a coat
on a boat that floats
in the MOAT
WHILE
a DAFT GIRAFFE
stands on a RAFT
and
LAUGHS.

A MOOSE on the loose
and a GOOSE
share some juice.
And.....

Attila the GORILLA
drinks vanilla
sarsaparilla
under an umbrella.

LATER...
At the equator
we are happy
that the 'GATOR
swallowed
a potato
and NOT
the waiter.

H

Boris the HORSE
shows no remorse
when he races vs.
Doris the Tortoise
(of course).
Oh! Pour us a chorus
for Boris the HORSE.

Gina the HYENA
could play
the concertina
and cook
a fine cuisina
BUT
a lean and mean
HYENA
stepped in between
her weinas
and
her beanas.

I

The IGUANA
from GHANA
named DONNA
cried:
'I just wanna
sit in a sauna
and
eat a banana!'

J

In the month of May
on his way to play
Ray the JAY
loves to lay
in the hay
EVERYDAY
and
PRAY by the Bay

Mr. JAGUAR wonders where you are?
And there you are Mrs. Jaguar!
Not very far but in a car
stuck in the tar
of a quagmire!
Do inquire about hiring the SQUIRE
who'll get a wire
around a tire
and jar that car
right outta thar'
OR
inquire about
a BUYER.

K

Paula the KOALA
stood on a
very tall wall
unafraid to fall
with her doll
and a ball.
Poppa Paul
was appalled
and called her
from the hall
in the mall:
'Paula! Paula!
Do not fall
at ALL
OR
you'll end up
in the hospital.'

Lou the KANGAROO
stood in a queue
on the avenue
for FREE vegetable stew
with a BLUE Caribou
wearing one shoe.
They knew what to do
as they waited for stew
and just chewed
some bamboo.
What a HULLABALLOO
when they both
sneezed KER-CHOO
from standing
in the queue
In that
early morning dew.

How fitting that my little KITTEN
is smitten
with just sitting and knitting
a pair of
winter mittens.

L

The LION
sat sighing
and crying
and said
he was dying...
he was lying.

Sam the LAMB
was an artisan
who wore a tam
and ate
HAM and JAM
with ABRAHAM
the RAM
in the aquarium.

THEN
it was WHAM! and BAM!
Because
The FISH SWAM
and ate their
JAM and HAM.

Baby LLAMA
sat in his
pajamas
at the DOLLARAMA
and cried for
MAMA
and
OBAMA!

M

The miserable MOUSE
will douse the louse
in the house.
He will laugh and throw water
and yell: 'YES! I got'er!'

Though its cold
eccentric MOLE
is on a roll.
His name is Joel
and he's up a pole
and
plays a role as
a silly soul.
He sold some gold
to a wealthy Toad
on the road
and
we are told
that Joel likes
to bowl in a hole
with coal.

The MULE
is a jewel
when in a pool
BUT
a fool
as a rule
in school.

AAH!

N

Toot! Toot!
What an absolute hoot
is the NEWT
who lives in my boot,
and plays the flute,
tickles my foot,
eats arrowroot
and is so cute
in his bathing suit.

O

He's just an OWL
who uttered
a VOWEL.
It was foul.
If you take a towel
to wipe his jowl
for crying foul
he'll HOWL!

Mrs. OTTER	Daughter met
caught her daughter	a handsome potter
In hot water.	who sought her
She took her	and caught her.
to her	Now they live
alma mater	in colder water
where they taught her.	that he bought her.

The OCTOPUS
cussed and fussed
on the school bus.
Now what can
be WORSE
than a 'pus
without a
PURSE?

P

It's a fine sign
when the PORCUPINE
who I have in mind
is the kind
who likes to dine
on fine wine
from the vine
and he's all mine...
then a pup showed up
with a great big cup.

Can you hand
Amanda the PANDA
a pyjamas?
Then she'll bake
a huge muffin
for a PUFFIN.

The PIG
in a wig
will dance a jig
if you
feed him
a FIG
that is
OVERLY BIG.

Q

Gail the QUAIL
(who wore a veil)
and Dale the SNAIL
would never fail
to deliver the mail
in a pail
down the trail
to the jail

to visit
the WHALE
with the big tail.
BUT
They didn't fail
to get to bail
that happy WHALE.

It's quite the tale!

R

I see that Mr. RHINO
is a fine albino.
He doesn't know
he doesn't show
in the snow.
ALSO
he doesn't know
he has a bow
tied on his toe
because it is low.
If RHINO were to know
might cause him woe –
so don't tell Moe
his dreaded foe
who lives in a
nearby bungalow.

The ROOSTER
got a BOOSTER
when he tasted
WORCESTERSHIRE.

HOUSE
OF
MOE
AAH!

S

Heidi the SPIDER

drank lots of cider

and only got wider.

She worked

as a GUIDE

but couldn't

hide her WIDE

OR

get lighter

AND

her clothes

just got tighter.

It's so sweet
to see the SHEEP
creep into a jeep
without a peep
after a
good night's sleep.

BUT
The sheep will weep
when that jeep
springs a leak.
Yet the sheep
will keep
the heap
because its
such a treat
to keep a
BEEP! BEEP! JEEP.

T

If the milk curdles,
Myrtle the TURTLE
should hurdle
her girdle
at Tina the TIGER,
who thinks she is wiser
but SHE IS NEITHER
... a morning riser
NOR a milk miser.

Who can buy a pan
from an old man
other than
a TOUCAN?

Why –
Dan can
Lou can
Sue can
and
YOU CAN!

Uncle TOAD
just sat and sewed
near his commode
at his adobe.
Then...
he caught a COAD
and couldn't blow
his noad.
Uncle TOAD
then showed
his nose
to his betrothed.

She said:
'It growed sweet TOAD
Your nose has growed!
It might explode –
It might erode!'
TOAD moaned:
'It's such a load
to have a nose that's growed.'

AND SO....
They rode to Dr. Spode
who sewed his nose
until it glowed.
He showed that toad
again a nose
in the mode
of a TOAD.

U

The UMBRELLA BIRD
is a little
ABSURD
as the word we've heard
is that he
...PURRED.

V

VIPER the piper
got all hyper
when he changed
a riper diaper
and forgot
to wipe'er.

Has Miss VULTURE any culture?
Only when you don't insult her.

W

Doreen the WOLVERINE
as a teen
in blue jeans
has always been keen
to be a college dean.
But
she's been seen
to be extremely mean.
It's in her genes
as a WOLVERINE.

The WORM is firm
and likes to squirm.
He yearns to learn
about
BIRD GERMS.

Wally WOODPECKER
on a double-decker
will wreck your deck
in a sec
with just one peck.
WELL-HECK!
Let's wring his neck!

Hi GUY!
The WALLEYE
that you buy
would rather
try to fly
than
FRY and DIE.

X

Mrs. Lynx
thinks she's a SPHINX
but Mr. Lynx
just winks and thinks
his ex is the best yet!

Y

It's a fact
that Jack the YAK
had a sore back
from carrying his pack.
Then he saw a
GREAT BIG TACK
in his sack-
gave it a WHACK
and NOW
he lacks the tack
AND the sore back.
YAY JACK!

Z

It's all been said
It's all been read
so now...
Let's put our ZED
to BED.

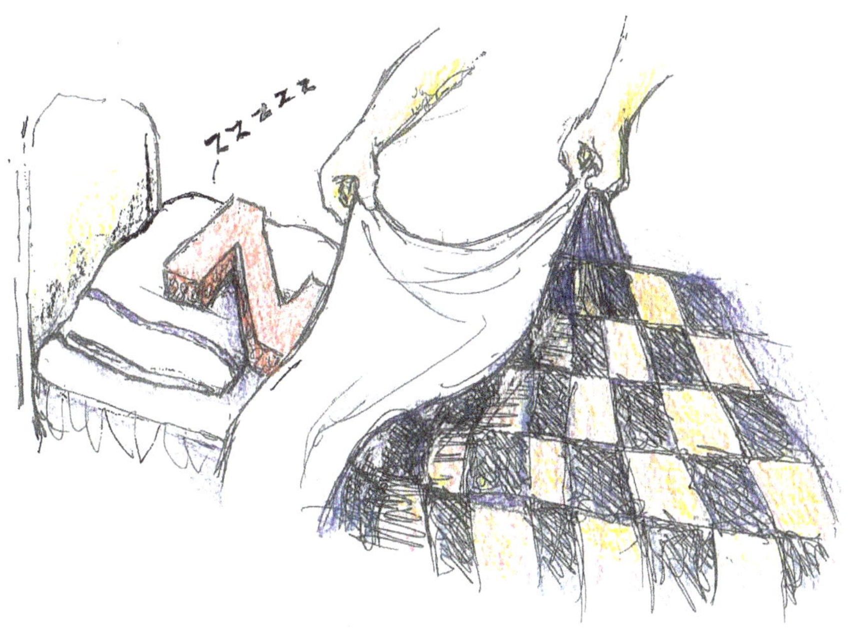

ZZZZZ

THE END!